Lucia's Travel Bus

Written by Nam-joong Kim
Illustrated by Eun-min Jeong
Edited by Joy Cowley

big & SMALL

Lucia lived in busy Santiago,
but every Saturday morning
her mother took her out of the city
to her grandfather's vineyard.
Grandpa grew grapes on the hillside.
He planted red roses near the grapes
that produced red wine,
and white roses near the grapes
that produced white wine.
If the roses withered, it meant
that the grapes had a disease.

2

Red wine is made with red grapes in their skins.
White wine is produced using green grapes without their skins.

3

4

Grandpa gave Lucia a hug.
"I have something to show you, chicita*."
He took her to the back of the house
where there was a sturdy yellow bus
with big wheels. "Look!" he said.
"This is Lucia's travel bus.
We will go to the end of the world."

* Chicita is the Spanish word for a little girl.

The southern end of Chile is sometimes called "the end of the world."
The village at the southernmost part of Chile is Puerto Toro.

5

Grandpa and Lucia set off in the bus,
traveling south toward the tip of Chile.
Inside the yellow bus were two beds
and a very small kitchen
where they could cook their meals.

Lucia asked Grandpa why he wanted
to go to the end of the world,
and he replied,
"All my life I have grown grapes
and made wine. Going to the end
of the world has been my dream
ever since I was your age.
What will we find there?
Let's go and see!"

Farther south, the weather got colder.
Wind blew and snowflakes flew around.
Grandpa gave Lucia a goose-down jacket,
a scarf, and a hat to keep her warm.
Lucia looked at the Andes mountain range
that stretched along the horizon to her left.
The peaks were covered in snow.

At night, when cold winds shook the bus,
Lucia wanted to go somewhere warm.
"Grandpa, what's in the north of Chile?"

"There is the Atacama Desert," he said.
"It gets less than an inch of rain a year,
and it is a very hot, dry place."

In some parts of the Atacama Desert it has never rained. The desert
has unusual colors because chemicals that are soluble, like iodine
and sulphur, are never washed out by rainfall.

Andes Mountains

Atacama Desert

Mount Aconcagu

Santiago

Chile

Pacific
Ocean

Lucia looked at Grandpa's old map
and saw how long Chile was.
The east side was blocked by the Andes.
The west side met the Pacific Ocean.

The yellow bus traveled on winding roads
through valleys with tall peaks on each side.

Paraguay

Uruguay

Argentina

Patagonia

Puerto Toro

After several days of travel,
they arrived at the end of the world.
This was where the road ended
and the ocean began – a place
where the sea and mountains
came together.

Penguins wandered around the lonely beach.
They stared at Lucia and she stared at them.

The yellow bus headed for home.
The wind got weaker, the air grew warmer.
Green orchards and fields could be seen.
Lucia sang a song and Grandpa listened.

When she got back home, Lucia said,
"Now I want to go to the Atacama Desert!"

Mom and Dad shook their heads.
"Grandpa is sick. We'll all go together
when he is feeling better."

Lucia couldn't wait to hear from Grandpa.
"If the Atacama Desert is too far,
maybe we can go to the Andes Mountains."

Grandpa's voice was weak. "Sure," he said.
"Let's go to see the Andes before it's too late."

This time Dad drove the yellow bus,
and Grandpa sat beside him.
After a long journey to the east,
they saw a tall peak against the sky.
It was Aconcagua, the tallest mountain
in the Andes mountain range.

 Aconcagua is the tallest mountain in the South American continent.
Although it is in Argentina, its western part borders Chile.

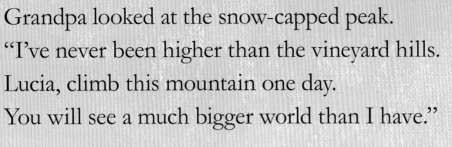

Grandpa looked at the snow-capped peak.
"I've never been higher than the vineyard hills.
Lucia, climb this mountain one day.
You will see a much bigger world than I have."

Lucia wanted to remember this moment.
She would come back to the mountain one day.

A month later, Grandpa passed away.
Lucia sat in the driver's seat of the yellow bus.
One day she would drive the travel bus
and then she'd climb up the highest peak.
The Aconcagua mountain was so close to heaven
she would probably hear Grandpa's voice.
"I'm coming, Grandpa," she whispered.

About Chile
The Long, Slender Country

The Chilean flag was designed in 1817. It has a long history compared with other countries' flags. The white represents the snow-covered Andes. The blue symbolizes Chilean skies. Red is for the blood spilt for independence and the white star refers to Chile's development.

A Belt or a Snake?

Chile is very long, but very narrow. From north to south it is approximately 2,650 miles (4,265 kilometers) – one of the longest countries in the world.

Andes Mountains, the Backbone of Chile

The length of the Andes mountain range is approximately 4,349 miles (7,000 kilometers). The longest mountain range in the world, it goes through several South American countries and is the second tallest after the Himalayas. The Andes has over 50 peaks that reach above 20,340 feet (6,200 meters). The tallest, the Aconcagua mountain, is in Argentina – although its western slopes are in Chile, so the mountain is the border between the two countries.

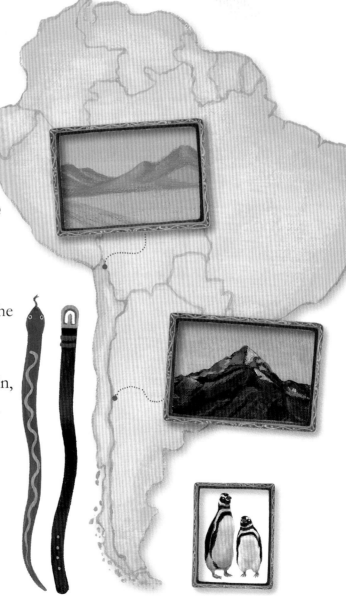

Santiago's Foggy Sky

The Pacific coast of South America has seasonal water-laden fogs caused by ocean currents and the mountains. In the garua (dry) season the fogs called camanchacas are thick and impede air traffic in Santiago. Extensive research has gone into plans to harvest the water vapor in the fogs, to benefit people living in desert areas.

A view of Santiago city from San Cristóbal Hill.

Different Climates, Different Scenery

As Chile is very long, its natural environment is diverse. In the north lies the Atacama Desert, and in the center is rich soil. Patagonia, at the southern tip of Chile, is cold, windy and has heavy rain. This means that three-quarters of its electricity is generated through hydropower. In the southern part of the Atacama Plateau are the San José mines. In 2010, 33 mine workers were trapped 2,290 feet (700 meters) underground for 69 days before being rescued. While they were trapped, their families sent down letters, books and phones in a capsule.

Rapel Dam and hydroelectric power station in central Chile

The Atacama Desert in the north

e landscape of Torres del Paine National Park in Patagonia

Easter Island is Full of Mysteries

Easter Island is in the South Pacific, west of the Chilean coastline. There are about 550 stone Moai statues on this island, carved by early ancestors of the indigenous Polynesian people. The statues have large heads with long ears, and they range in size from 6 to 100 feet (2 to 30 meters) tall. They were quarried from one volcanic area on the island, but it is not known when they were made or how they were moved to stand as sentinels around the coast.

Some of the Moai statues of Easter Island (Isla de Pascua), Chile

Copper and Fish

Chile is a country of rich resources. It has a quarter of the world's copper and is the number one exporter of the metal, which gets made into coins, pipes or electric wires. Because Chile has a long coastline, it has access to sea resources. It exports the most fish powder in the world, which is made into fertilizers and animal food. In the southern fjords, Chile has salmon farms and exports salmon to many countries, including the USA.

Chuquicamata, one of the biggest copper mines in the world.

Chile's Wine Export

The temperature difference between day and night is wide, and this aids the ripening of grapes for wine. Thanks to the clear water from the Andes Mountains and the rich soil, Chile's vineyards thrive, producing wine that is sold around the world. Chilean red wines are considered as good as European wines but are not as expensive.

northern hemisphere

equator

southern hemisphere

Chilean Table Grapes

Countries in the northern hemisphere have seasons opposing those of the southern hemisphere, so in the northern winter and spring, grapes from Chile's late summer and fall are a welcome fruit.

Chilean vineyard in the foothills of the Andes

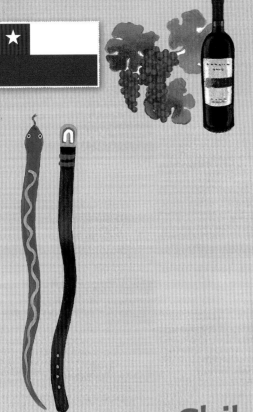

Chile

Name: Republic of Chile

Location: South-west region of South America

Area: 470,347 mi^2 (756,950 km^2)

Capital: Santiago

Population: Approx. 17.6 million (2014)

Language: Spanish

Religion: Catholic (Christianity)

Main exports: Copper, paper and pulp, fruit, wine

Bolivia

Arica

Atacama Desert

Calama

Brazil

Paraguay

*Wine
One of the world famous
products of Chile

Argentina

Uruguay

*Moai
The stone statues shaped like
human faces on Easter Island

Pacific Ocean

Santiago

*La Moneda Palace
The office of the President
of the Republic of Chile

*Viña del Mar
A major resort city on
central Chile's Pacific coast

Concepcion

*Chile

Atlantic Ocean

*Condor
The largest flying land birds that live
only in South America

*Quena (or Kena)
The traditional flute of the Andes,
made of bamboo or wood

Punta Arenas

Puerto Toro
The "end of the world"

Original Korean text by Nam-joong Kim
Illustrations by Eun-min Jeong
Korean edition © Aram Publishing

This English edition published by big & SMALL in 2016
by arrangement with Aram Publishing
English text edited by Joy Cowley
English edition © big & SMALL 2016

Distributed in the United States and Canada by
Lerner Publishing Group, Inc.
241 First Avenue North
Minneapolis, MN 55401 U.S.A.
www.lernerbooks.com

Images by page no. - left to right, top to bottom
Page 26: © David Berkowitz (CC-BY-SA-2.0); © Avodrocc (CC-BY-2.0);
public domain; © refractor (Flickr) (CC-BY-2.0); Page 28: public domain;
© Reinhard Jahn, Mannheim (CC-BY-SA-2.0); © Beatrice Murch (CC-BY-SA-2.0)

ISBN: 978-1-925247-28-2

Printed in Korea